Google Pixel 8 & 8
Pro User Guide

The Comprehensive Step-by-Step
Instruction and Illustrated Manual for
Beginners & Seniors to Master the Google
Pixel 8 and 8 Pro with Tips and Tricks

Shawn Blaine

Table of Contents

Introduction

The Google Pixel lineup is one of the best Android smartphones. The company has integrated a matte finish for the Pixel 8 Pro, although its camera bar and frame still retain the brushed aluminum, whereas the Pixel 8 features a matte aluminum frame, but the back is furnished with glossy glass.

Google has upgraded the camera configuration of the Pixel 8 series. The lenses are now packed closer together, and there's a temperature sensor that can measure the temperature of objects and surfaces.

While the Pixel 8 has a 6.2-inch display, the Pro model incorporates a 6.7-inch display, with the screen now looking sharper and brighter. It's also good to mention that the Pixel 8 adopts a 1080p resolution, whereas Google has implemented a 1440p LTPO OLED panel for the Pro model.

Also, Google has incorporated the new Tensor G3 processor for both devices, and the AI capability of the device stands to benefit from this inclusion. The standard Pixel 8 features 8GB of RAM with a storage capacity of 128GB or 256GB, while the company has adopted 12GB of RAM for the Pro model with a storage option of 512GB or 1TB.

The Pixel 8 series features some stunning cameras and AI capabilities.

Google has revamped the three camera sensors for the Pro model but only implemented a new main sensor for the regular Pixel 8. However, the 50MP lens remains the same for the two devices and features a revamped f/1.68 aperture. Google has renewed the ultrawide and periscope telephoto lenses for only the Pro model, and only the Pro model supports autofocus.

The Pixel 8 series supports capturing Night Sight photos, and thanks to the improved software, Google has implemented Magic Editor, Best Take for photos, and Video Boost for shooting videos.

As expected, the Pixel 8 series will ship with Android 14 and will also receive 7 years of complete operating system updates.

Google Assistant is now able to summarize and reword displayed information, accelerate voice typing, and even fetch more information via At a Glance.

If you're searching for a manual to help you master and operate your Google Pixel 8 series, then look no further, as this guide has been written to help you learn how to use and operate your Google Pixel 8 and 8 Pro at an expert level. This user manual is designed with step-by-step instructions and helpful screenshots to make it simpler and easier to navigate and operate your Google Pixel efficiently and comfortably.

This user manual will help you get started with your Google Pixel 8 series and also serve as your reference and go-to manual, regardless of whether you're a beginner or a pro.

Chapter One

Set up Google Pixel

After you've purchased your Google Pixel smartphone, ensure you've charged it fully before attempting to power it on and then set it up.

- To set up, start by inserting your 5G SIM into the device.
- After that, long-tap the Power key until the Google icon displays on the screen, then let go.
- Once the "**Welcome to your Pixel**" menu shows up, proceed by choosing your desired language.
- Now, choose "**Get started**."

- Next up, select "**Continue**" underneath the "**Phone activation**" menu.
- While on the "**Connect to Wi-Fi**" interface, choose a network. Afterward, input the network's password to proceed.
- Once you get to the "**Copy apps & data**" interface, go ahead and choose "**Next**" or the "**Don't Copy**" option as per your preference.

Don't copy   Next

- Proceed by inserting your Google email address on the **"Sign in"** menu.

- After that, choose "**Next**."
- From the resulting "**Google Services**" menu, choose your preferred options.
- After that, choose "**Accept**."

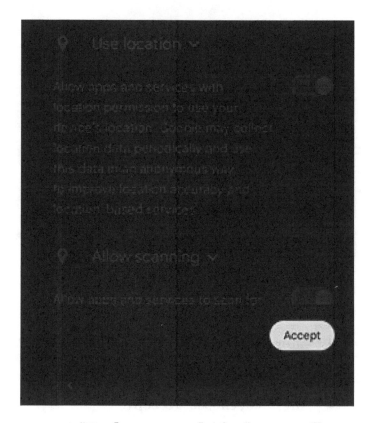

- A "**Back up your device**" menu will appear; select "**Turn on**" to commence backing up instantly, or select "**Not now**" to do it later.

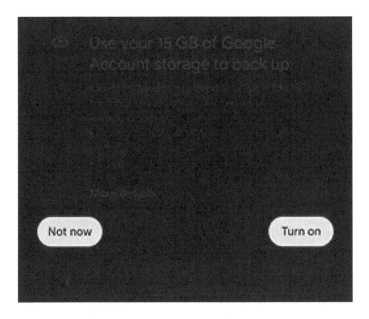

- On the Services menu, choose an option and then select "**I accept**."
- From there, select "**Next**."
- On the "**Legal Terms**" menu, hit on "**I accept**."
- While on the "**Set a PIN**" menu, go ahead and input your desired PIN code.
- Now, select "**Next**."
- You'll be shown the "**Continue setup?**" menu; choose "**Continue**" to completely configure and customize your smartphone. If you need to finish up later, select "**Leave & get reminder**."

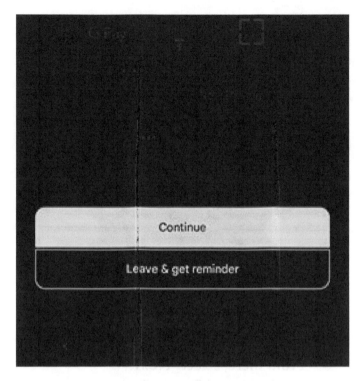

- Under the "**Google hands-free**" menu, review the information. After that, choose "**I agree**" to configure Google Assistant. To do it later, choose "**Skip**."
- Next up, select "**I agree**" or "**Skip**."
- Once you arrive at the "**Anything else**" menu, go ahead and set up more features or "**No thanks**."
- After that, choose "**Yes, I'm in**" or "**No thanks**."
- Next up, hit on "**Try it**."
- Once you get to the "**All set!**" menu, go ahead and swipe upward from the bottom to access the Home screen.

Backup & Restore

- Launch the Settings app.
- Next, choose "**System**."
- Then choose "**Backup**."
- When asked, select "**Turn on**" to activate Backup.
- Next up, press the "**Backup by Google One**" toggle to enable or disable it.
- While on the "**Account storage**" box, go ahead and list the necessary email address.
- If you need to change accounts, press "**Account storage**."
- Go ahead and choose the desired account or select "**Add account**."

Restart Google Pixel

- Long-tap the Power and Volume up keys until a context menu shows up.
- Then choose "**Restart**."

Set up eSIM

Ensure you confirm if your carrier supports eSIM before you proceed.

- Launch the Settings app.
- Next up, choose "**Network & Internet**."

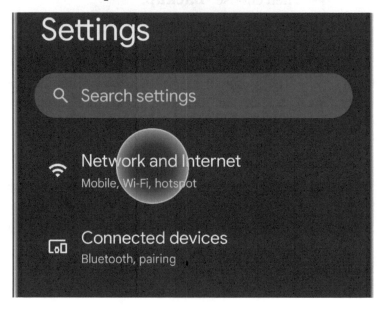

- From there, choose "**SIMs**."

- After this, choose **"Download a SIM instead?"**

- Then hit on "**Next**.

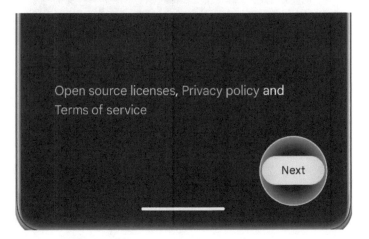

- Go through the displayed prompts to finish.

Insert SIM Card

Once you've inserted a nano SIM card, you can connect your Google Pixel to a mobile network.

- Take out your SIM ejection instrument and insert it into the tiny hole (SIM tray) on the lower left corner of your smartphone.

- Proceed by carefully pushing the tiny hole with the instrument until it ejects the SIM tray.

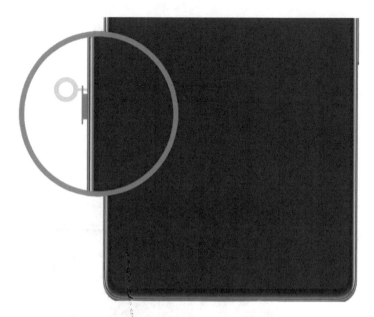

- Then remove the SIM tray once it comes out.

- Follow up by placing your physical SIM card into the tray.
- Carefully place the tray back into its position and hold on for your Google Pixel to automatically detect the SIM card.

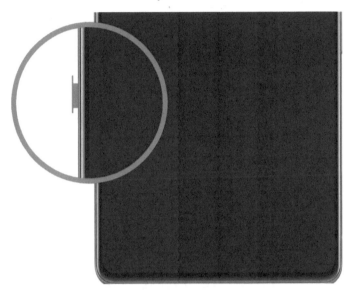

Add SIM PIN

Once you enable SIM PIN, your SIM card will only be unlocked when you insert the correct code.

- Launch the Settings app.
- Next up, hit "**Security & privacy**."
- After that, hit "**Advanced settings**."
- From there, hit "**SIM card lock**."

- Now, hit the **"Lock SIM card"** toggle to enable it.
- Proceed by entering the current SIM PIN.
- Now, choose **"OK."**

However, if you need to change the SIM PIN:

- Hit on **"Change SIM PIN."**
- Follow up by entering and re-entering the existing SIM PIN.
- Now, choose **"OK."**
- Go ahead and insert your new SIM PIN.
- Now, choose **"OK."**
- Proceed by re-entering the new SIM PIN.
- Now, choose **"OK."**

Enable Bluetooth

Once you have Bluetooth enabled on your Google Pixel smartphone, it'll become visible to other devices.

- While on your home screen, swipe upward to reveal your apps.
- Select the Settings app.
- After this, choose **"Connected devices."**
- Next up, select **"Connection preferences."**
- From there, select **"Bluetooth."**
- Proceed by tapping the **"Use Bluetooth"** toggle to enable or disable it.

View Battery History

- While on your home screen, swipe upward to reveal your apps.
- Select the Settings app.
- Then choose "**Battery**."
- From here, you can evaluate your battery status.
- Hit on "**Battery usage**."
- Go through the "**Advanced battery**" use information.
- From the "**Battery history**" chart, you can review the phone's battery level for the last twenty-four hours.

Enable Power Saver

Battery saver restricts certain features and services, such as location services and background apps, to enhance the phone's battery life.

- While on your home screen, swipe upward to reveal your apps.
- Select the Settings app.
- Then choose "**Battery**."
- After this, choose "**Battery saver**."

- Proceed by tapping the toggle next to the "**Use Battery saver**" option to ⬤ enable or ⬤ disable it.
- Next up, choose "**Set a schedule**."
- After that, choose from the options.
- Hit on "**Turn off when charged**" to ⬤ enable or ⬤ disable it when your Google Pixel is fully charged.

Change Device Language

- Launch the Settings app.
- Then choose "**System**."
- Next up, choose "**Languages & input**."
- Now, hit on "**Languages**."
- Proceed by selecting "**Add a language**."
- Go ahead and choose the appropriate language.

Chapter Two

Manage Data Settings

This section shows you how to enable and configure your data and Wi-Fi services on your Google Pixel.

Enable Data

- Launch the Settings app.
- Then choose "**Network & internet**."
- Next, choose "**SIMs**."
- Proceed by tapping the toggle next to "**Mobile data**" to enable or disable it.
- When prompted, choose "**OK**."

Enable Data Roaming

If you're embarking on international travel, confirming your device's data roaming settings is important.

- Launch the Settings app.
- Then choose "**Network & internet**."
- Next, choose "**SIMs**."
- After this, press the "**Roaming**" toggle to enable or disable it.
- When prompted, select "**OK**."

Enable Mobile Data Warning

When your data consumption reaches the set threshold, an alert will display.

- Launch the Settings app.
- Then choose "**Network & internet**."
- Next, choose "**SIMs**."
- From there, choose "**Data warning & limit**."
- Next up, choose "**Set data warning**" to enable it.
- Then choose "**Data warning**."
- Proceed by entering your desired warning limit.
- After that, select "**Set**."

Add Mobile Data Limit

Once your data usage reaches the set data usage limit, as shown by the red line, mobile data will be disabled on your Google Pixel unless you manually adjust it or use a Wi-Fi connection.

- Launch the Settings app.
- Then choose "**Network & internet**."
- Next, choose "**SIMs**."
- From there, choose "**Data warning & limit**."
- Next up, choose "**Set data limit**" to enable it.
- If you're shown the "**Limiting data usage**" menu, go through the message and press "**OK**."

- After that, choose "**Data limit**."
- Proceed by entering your desired data usage limit.
- Next up, press "**Set**."

Enable Data Saver

- Launch the Settings app.
- Then choose "**Network & internet**."
- From there, select "**Data Saver**."
- Next up, press the "**Use Data Saver**" toggle to enable or disable it.

Enable Wi-Fi

Sometimes you may prefer to use a Wi-Fi connection instead of mobile data on your Google Pixel.

- Launch the Settings app.
- From there, hit "**Network & internet**."
- Hit on "**Internet**."
- Now, hit the "**Wi-Fi**" toggle to enable or disable it.

Enable Wi-Fi Hotspot

- Launch the Settings app.
- From there, hit "**Network & internet**."
- After this, hit "**Hotspot & tethering**."
- Next up, hit "**Wi-Fi hotspot**."

- Now, hit **"Use Wi-Fi hotspot"** to enable or disable it.
- Then choose **"OK."**

Disable Wi-Fi Connection

- Launch the Settings app.
- Now, choose **"Network & internet."**
- Afterward, choose **"Internet."**
- Proceed by long-tapping the Wi-Fi network.
- Then choose **"Forget."**

Change Network Mode

- Launch the Settings app.
- Now, choose **"Network & internet."**
- Afterward, choose **"SIMs."**
- Next up, choose **"Preferred network type."**
- Proceed by selecting **"5G"** or **"LTE."**

Change Wi-Fi Hotspot Password

You can remove your current mobile or Wi-Fi hotspot password and enter a new one if you feel the previous one is compromised.

- Launch the Settings app.
- Now, choose "**Network & internet**."
- After this, hit "**Hotspot & tethering**."
- Next up, choose "**Wi-Fi hotspot**."
- Proceed by tapping the **Hotspot password** box and entering your desired password.
- Afterward, choose "**OK**."

Automatically Switch between Wi-Fi and Mobile Data Network

- Launch the Settings app.
- Now, choose "**Network & internet**."
- After this, hit "**Internet**."
- Next up, choose "**Network preferences**."

- After that, press "**Switch to mobile data automatically**" to enable or disable it.

Connect to a Wi-Fi Network

Before attempting to connect to Wi-Fi, ensure that you have your Wi-Fi enabled.

- Launch the Settings app.
- Now, choose "**Network & internet**."
- After this, hit "**Internet**."
- While on the "**Wi-Fi networks**" header, choose your desired network.
- When asked, insert the password.
- Now, choose "**Connect**."

Set up a Virtual Private Network

A virtual private network, which is abbreviated as "VPN," allows you to encrypt Google Pixel internet traffic and secure your web identity; this is achieved thanks to an encrypted remote server.

- Launch the Settings app.

- Now, choose "**Network & internet**."
- Afterward, hit "**VPN**."
- Then select the **Add button** ✚.
- When shown a lock screen alert, hit on "**OK**."
- Proceed by entering the required name underneath the "**Name**" box.
- Under the "**Type field**," select the **Dropdown menu**.
- Follow up by choosing the VPN type.
- Follow up by inserting the needed information into the applicable box.
- Now, choose "**Save**."

Chapter Three

Manage your Email

Just like every smartphone, you can manage your Google and other preferred mail services on your Google Pixel.

Adding an Email Account

- Launch the Settings app.
- From there, choose "**Passwords & accounts**."
- Next up, choose "**Add account**."
- From the resulting menu, select your email provider or IT admin.
- Proceed by entering your Email address.
- Now, select "**Next**."
- Go ahead and insert the Password and choose "**Sign in**."
- On the "**Terms & Conditions**" menu, select "**Yes**" to proceed.
- Follow up by entering the required information, then select "**Next**."
- If shown, choose "**Advanced**" to double-check that the certificate is correct.
- After that, choose "**Proceed Anyway**."
- On the next menu, insert the required information and press "**Next**."

- Proceed by customizing the account options and adding a name, then select "**Next**."

Sync your Email

- Launch the Settings app.
- From there, choose "**Passwords & accounts**."
- Then choose the email address and select "**Account sync**."
- Proceed by tapping the needed data sync options such as Calendar, Contacts, etc., to enable or disable them.

For manual sync:

- Hit on the **Menu button** ⋮ at the upper-right.
- Then select "**Sync now**."

Delete Email Account

- Launch the Settings app.
- From there, choose "**Passwords & accounts**."
- Then choose the Gmail account.
- Now, choose "**Remove account**."
- Then select "**Remove account**" once more.

Adding an Existing Google Account

- While on your home screen, swipe upward to reveal your apps.
- Select the Settings app.
- Next up, hit on **"Passwords & accounts."**
- Now, choose **"Add account."**
- After that, select **"Google."**
- When asked, insert your security method (for instance, password, fingerprint, etc.) to proceed.
- Proceed by entering your Gmail address.
- After that, select **"Next."**
- Go ahead and input the password, then choose **"Next."**
- From there, choose **"Yes, I'm in"** to use your phone number in updating the account or **"Skip"** to ignore.
- Go through the **"Service & Privacy Policy."** After that, choose **"I agree."**
- Proceed by turning on or off the following: settings, Wi-Fi passwords, app data, etc., by checking them.
- Swipe upward from the bottom to close the menu.

Chapter Four

Set up Screen Lock

Adding a PIN, password and other screen lock type protects your Google Pixel so that only you and someone who has your password or PIN can unlock the device.

Add Pattern

Once you've set up an unlock pattern on your Google Pixel, you'll need to use that pattern to unlock your device after its screen locks.

- Launch the Settings app.
- After that, hit "**Security & privacy**."
- Then hit on "**Screen lock**."
- When asked, go ahead and add a Google account. Hit on "**Add Google**" if you've not done so before now.
- Hit on "**Continue**" to move ahead without adding a Google account.
- When prompted, insert your current lock type.
- Then select "**Pattern**."
- Proceed by drawing an unlock pattern by connecting multiple dots.
- After that, hit "**Next**."
- Follow up by drawing the same pattern once more.
- Now, select "**Confirm**."

- When asked, choose any of the options and select "**OK**."

Add PIN

For people who prefer using numbers for unlocking their device, the PIN lock type should be selected. This allows you to insert four to sixteen numerics that will be used in unlocking your Google Pixel.

- Launch the Settings app.
- Next up, hit "**Security & privacy**."
- Then hit on "**Screen lock**."
- When asked, go ahead and add a Google account. Hit on "**Add Google**" if you've not done so before now.
- Hit on "**Continue**" to move ahead without adding a Google account.
- When prompted, insert your current lock type.
- Then select "**PIN**."
- Proceed by entering your numeric PIN.
- Now, choose "Next."
- Follow up by re-entering the PIN.
- Now, select "**Confirm**."
- Afterward, select "**OK**."

Add Password

To unlock your Google Pixel using a password, you'll need to insert a combination of both numbers and alphabets, including symbols.

- Launch the Settings app.
- Next up, hit "**Security & privacy**."
- Then hit on "**Screen lock**."
- When asked, go ahead and add a Google account. Hit on "**Add Google**" if you've not done so before now.
- Hit on "**Continue**" to move ahead without adding a Google account.
- When prompted, insert your current lock type.
- Then select "**Password**."
- Proceed by entering a password.
- Now, choose "**Next**."
- Follow up by re-entering the password.
- After that, choose "**Confirm**."
- When asked, choose from the displayed options and hit "**OK**."

Remove Screen Lock

If you prefer to use your smartphone without using any lock type, then you can disable them.

- Launch the Settings app.
- Next up, hit "**Security & privacy**."
- Then hit on "**Screen lock**."
- Hit on "**Continue**."
- Proceed by entering your existing PIN, and password/pattern.
- After that, hit on "**None**" or "**Swipe**."
- Next up, choose "**Yes, remove**."

Add Fingerprints Unlock

If you prefer to use your fingerprints for biometrics and unlock your Google Pixel, then you can enable it.

- Launch the Settings app.
- Now, choose "**Security & privacy**."
- After this, hit on "**Face & Fingerprint Unlock**."
- When asked, go ahead and insert your current password/pattern.
- Next, choose "**Fingerprint Unlock**."
- From there, select "**Add fingerprint**."
- Proceed by placing your finger on your Google Pixel sensor until it buzzes then let go.
- Go ahead and repeat these steps as required until it's complete.
- Afterward, choose "**Done**."

Delete Fingerprints

- Launch the Settings app.
- Now, choose "**Security & privacy**."
- After this, hit on "**Face & Fingerprint Unlock**."
- When asked, go ahead and insert your current password/pattern.
- Next, choose "**Fingerprint Unlock**."

- Next up, hit on the Delete button 🗑 next to the fingerprint you intend to delete.
- Afterward, choose "**Delete**."

Add Face Recognition

Just as you can use fingerprints for biometrics and unlock your Google Pixel, you can do the same with face recognition.

- Launch the Settings app.
- From there, hit on "**Security & privacy**."

- Next up, hit on "**Face & Fingerprint Unlock**."
- When asked, insert your current password/pattern.
- Afterward, choose "**Face Unlock**."

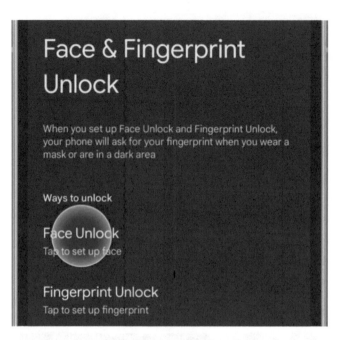

- Next up, choose **"I agree."**

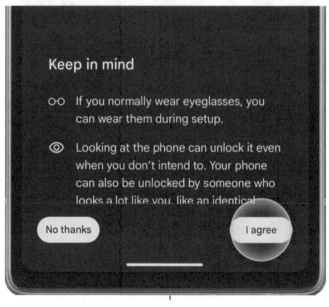

- Then select **"Start."**

- From the resulting menu, go through the info and select "**I agree**." Or select "**Skip**" to skip it.
- Ensure you hold your smartphone about eight or fifteen inches away and place your face within the camera view as shown on the screen.
- On the "**Looks good!**" menu, choose "**Done**."

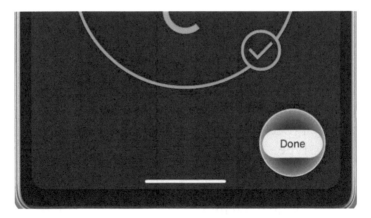

Delete Face Data

- Launch the Settings app.

- From there, hit on **"Security & privacy**."
- Next up, hit on **"Face & Fingerprint Unlock**."
- When asked, insert your current password/pattern.
- Afterward, choose **"Face Unlock**."
- Next up, choose **"Delete**."
- Go through the disclaimer and select **"Delete**."

Set up Smart Lock

With Smart Lock turned on, your Google Pixel will automatically unlock whenever it is in a trusted location or it detects other devices/accessories. However, you must have lock type enabled on your Google Pixel for Smart Lock to work.

- Launch the Settings app.
- Now, hit on **"Security & privacy**."
- Next up, choose **"Advanced settings**."
- After this, choose **"Smart Lock**."
- Proceed by entering your current unlock type.
- Follow up by choosing the available options and going through the onscreen guide to enable a trusted unlock. You can toggle on **"On-body detection"** so that your Google Pixel will remain unlocked whenever it's in your bag or pocket. Or **"Trusted places"** to ensure that your

smartphone is unlocked anytime you're in the specified location. Or "**Trusted devices**" to unlock your Google Pixel when certain accessories or gadgets are connected.

Chapter Five

Set up a Conference Call

- While on your home screen, swipe upward to reveal your apps.
- Launch the Phone app.
- Then select the Keypad icon ⦂⦂.
- Proceed by inserting the number, then select "**Call**."
- If you need to choose the phone number from your contacts, select "**Contacts**." After that, choose a contact. Follow up by tapping the number.
- After the call connects, select "**Add call**."
- Go ahead and input a ten-digit number.
- Afterward, select "**Call**."
- After the call connects, choose "**Merge**."

Enable Video Calling

- Launch the Phone app.
- Then select the Menu button ⦂ on the upper-right.
- From there, select "**Settings**."
- Next up, choose "**Calling accounts**."
- Proceed by selecting your network if you're using a physical SIM/eSIM.

- Follow up by tapping the toggle beside the "**Turn on video calling**" option to enable or disable it.
- If prompted, read the alert and select "**OK**."

Remove Call History

- Launch the Phone app.
- From there, hit on the "**Recents**" tab to reveal your call history.
- Then select the Menu button ⋮ on the upper-right.
- After this, select "**Call History**."
- Then select the Menu button ⋮ once more.
- From there, choose "**Clear call history**."
- Next up, choose "**OK**."

Delete Call Log

- Launch the Phone app.
- From there, hit on the "**Recents**" tab to reveal your call history.
- Long-tap the call you intend to delete.
- Then choose "**Delete**."

Adding a Speed Dial

- Long-tap a blank section on your Home screen.
- Then choose "**Widgets**."
- Under the "**Contacts**" header, long-tap "**Direct dial**."
- Proceed by dragging the widget to your desired Home screen and let go.
- Then click on a contact. However, if the contact comprises of many numbers, choose the appropriate number.

Delete a Speed Dial

- Long-tap the "**Direct dial**" button.
- Proceed by dragging the widget up to "**Remove**" then let go.

Block & Unblock Numbers

Once you add a contact to your block list, their calls will be automatically ignored and end up in voicemail. Also, their text and photo messages will not appear in your Messages app.

Block a Number

- Launch the Phone app.
- Then select the Menu symbol.
- Next up, choose "**Settings**."
- From there, choose "**Blocked numbers**."
- After this, choose "**Add a number**."
- Proceed by adding the number you intend to block.
- Afterward, choose "**Block**."

Unblock a Number

- Launch the Phone app.
- Then select the Menu symbol.
- Next up, choose "**Settings**."
- From there, choose "**Blocked numbers**."
- Now, hit on the Close symbol ✕ next to the blocked number.
- Next up, choose "**Unblock**."

Make a Phone Call

- Launch the Phone app.
- From there, select the Keypad button ⦙⦙⦙.
- Proceed by inserting a phone number.

- After that, choose **"Call."**
- However, if you intend to choose a contact, hit on the **"Contacts"** tab on the bottom-right. Next up, choose the contact and click on their number to dial it.

Transfer Files to PC

- Hint: This method of file transfer only works for unencrypted files.
- Start by connecting your Google Pixel to a PC by using the accompanying USB cable.
- If needed, long-tap the Status bar which is located at the top, then go ahead and drag to the bottom.
- From there, select the Android system button which displays **"Charging this device via USB."**
- Next up, choose **"File transfer/Android Auto."**
- Proceed by copying the desired files from your PC.
- Head to the File Explorer on your PC.
- From the File Explorer on your PC, choose **"Pixel 8."**
- Next up, choose **"Internal shared storage."**
- Then paste the copied files on any of the desired folders on your smartphone's **"Internal shared storage."**

- Go ahead and unplug the USB cable from your PC once you're done.

Manage RTT Call

Once you have real-time text (RTT) enabled on your Google Pixel, you can see texts as they are being typed by the sender.

Adjust RTT Visibility

- Launch the Phone app.
- Now, press the Menu button ⋮ on the upper-right.
- Afterward, hit "**Settings**."
- Next up, hit "**Accessibility**."
- After this, hit on "**Real-time text (RTT)**."
- Proceed by choosing from the options on the resulting menu.

Phone Call with RTT

- Launch the Phone app and dial a number.
- After the call is connected, hit the **RTT button** . Or swipe towards the left to choose the **RTT button** .

End RTT Call

- During a call, hit the End button on the top left to disconnect.

Send Messages

With the Messages application on your Google Pixel, you'll be able to send images, media content, and text messages to anyone.

- Launch the Messages app.
- Then select "**Start chat**."

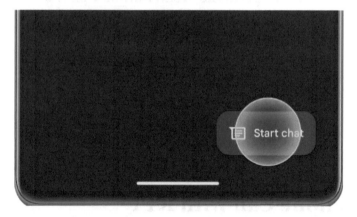

- Proceed by selecting a contact or inserting their phone number if they're not in your contacts list.
- If you need to begin a group message, hit on "**Create group**."

- Follow up by composing your message. If you desire to include an emoji, select "**Emoji** ."

- Afterward, hit on **Send** SMS.
- However, if you need to access your new message, swipe downward from the top of the display to reveal the alert, then click on the message. Right there, you can even reply to the message, and even mark it as read.

Chapter Six

Manage your Google Pixel Camera

With the Camera application, you can capture excellent images and videos by using an array of customization options.

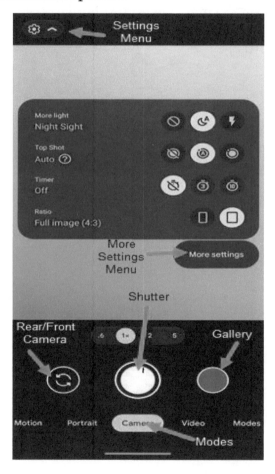

View Camera Settings

- While on your home screen, swipe upward to reveal your apps
- Then select the Camera app.
- From there, choose the **Settings Menu button** .
- Proceed by selecting an option and then toggle them on or off. The options include Timer, Gestures, Videos stabilization, Exposure, Camera photo resolution, etc.

Add Camera Timer

The timer enables you to choose the duration of the delay before your phone's camera captures a picture automatically.

- Launch the Camera app.
- Then select the **Settings Menu button** .
- From there, choose the **Timer button** to choose the duration of the delay: **10 seconds**, **Off**, or **3 seconds**.

Switch Camera

The camera switch enables you to alternate between the back and front cameras.

- Launch the Camera app.

- From there, select the **Camera Facing button** to alternate between the phone's back and front-facing camera.

Change Shooting Modes

The Google Pixel offers different shooting modes for the camera application and you can select an option depending on what you need to achieve.

- Launch the Camera app.
- To adjust your camera mode, swipe horizontally (right or left) to choose an option: Motion, Panorama, Portrait, Night Sight, etc.
- After selecting your desired mode, hit on the **Shutter button** to capture.

Capture with Night Sight

With the Night Sight mode, users can capture the finest information and colors when capturing images/videos at night.

- To use it, choose "**Night Sight**.

- After that, press **Capture**  .

Capture with Long Exposure

Long Exposure enables users to add artistic blur to their moving objects.

Once you're set to capture and blur a subject in motion, hit "**Long Exposure**."

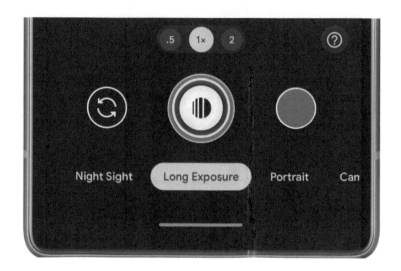

Use Magic Eraser

With the magic eraser, users can get rid of people and items from their images immediately.

- Navigate to the image you desire to edit.
- Now, choose **Edit**.
- Move to **Tools**. From there, choose "**Magic eraser**."
- Proceed by drawing a circle/doodle across the item you intend to delete.

Add Blur

With blur, you can adjust the focus section of your image.

- While customizing an image, move to **Tools**.
- Then select "Portrait blur."

- After this, choose **Blur**.
- Proceed by tapping the display to adjust the focus area. Then use the slider to make adjustments, if required.

Enable Quick Tap

Quick Tap enables users to launch the camera application from any menu by tapping twice on the back of their Google Pixel.

To enable Quick Tap:

- Launch the Settings app.
- After this, choose "**System**."
- Next up, choose "**Gestures**."
- Now, select "**Quick Tap**."
- Proceed by toggling on "**Use Quick Tap**."
- Afterward, hit "**Open app**."
- Now, hit "**Camera**."

Enable Flip Camera

Once you enable Flip Camera and your Camera application is open, you can switch between your phone's front and back cameras by twisting the phone two times.

To enable Flip Camera:

- Launch the Settings app.
- After this, choose "**System**."
- Then choose "**Gestures**."

- Proceed by toggling on "**Flip camera for selfie**."

Share Videos

- While on your home screen, swipe upward to reveal your apps.
- Then select the Photos app.
- From there, select an album.
- Long-tap a video.

- Next up, select the Share button.
- Under the "**Share via**" menu, go ahead and choose how you prefer to share the video (for instance, Gmail, Bluetooth, etc.). The next menu will vary depending on the selected option.
- So, go ahead and insert any additional information needed to share the content.

Capture & Share a Photo

- While on your home screen, swipe upward to reveal your apps
- Then select the Camera app.
- Hold your Pixel phone firmly and press anywhere on the display to focus.

- After that, press the Shutter button ⬤ to capture the image.
- Select the image thumbnail next to the Shutter button ⬤ to preview the photo.
- Then choose the Share button ◁ at the lower-left.
- Under the "**Share via**" menu, go ahead and choose how you prefer to share the photo (for instance, Gmail, Bluetooth, etc.). The next menu will vary depending on the selected option.
- So, go ahead and insert any additional information needed to share the content.

Capture & Share Videos

- While on your home screen, swipe upward to reveal your apps
- Then select the Camera app.
- From there, select "**Video**."
- Hold your Pixel phone firmly, then hit the **Record Video button** ⬤ and touch somewhere on the screen to focus.
- When you're done, select the **Stop button** ⭕ to end the recording.
- If you need to preview the video, hit the **Preview button**; it is the round icon

positioned on the right side of the record button.

- While on the preview menu, choose the

  Share button from the bottom-left.
- Proceed by selecting your desired sharing method (Messages, Bluetooth, etc.).

Capture a Screenshot

- If you need to capture a screenshot, long-tap the power and volume down keys at once.

Record & Play Sound Files

- While on your home screen, swipe upward to reveal your apps.
- Then select the **Recorder** app.
- Review the disclaimer (when prompted).
- After that, choose "**Get started**."
- From there, choose the **Record button**.
- If you need to pause your recording, select

  the Pause button .
- To resume recording after you've paused it, select **Resume**.

- Hit on "**Add title**" to insert the file's name.
- After that, choose "**Save**."
- If you need to play the file, click on it and select the Play button .
- If you need to remove the recording, hit the **Menu button** at the upper-right. From there, choose "**Delete**" two times to approve.

Chapter Seven

Contacts App

With the Contacts application, users can manage their calls and contacts.

Adding a Contact

- While on your home screen, swipe upward to reveal your apps
- Then select the Contacts app.
- If you intend to choose an account instead of the default, select the **Switch account button** 🅢 that is positioned at the top-right, then choose your preferred account.
- After that, choose the **Add button** 🞣 on the bottom-right.
- Proceed by inserting the email, number, etc., then hit "**Save**."

Remove a Contact

- Launch the Contacts app.
- Then choose a contact.
- Next up, select the **Menu button** ⋮ on the top-right.
- Now, choose "**Delete**."
- After that, choose "**Move to Trash**."

Editing your Contact

- Launch the Contacts app.
- Then choose a contact.
- From there, select the **Edit contact button** 🖊.
- Proceed by changing the email, phone number, and more.
- Once done, select "**Save**."
- If you need to adjust other options, select the **Dropdown menu** ▼ below the selection and choose your desired option.

Link your Contacts

Your Google Pixel automatically merges contact information from your email and phone book. However, if you notice a mistake, you can delete, customize, or undo the changes.

- Launch the Contacts app.
- Long-tap the first contact.
- Next up, tap the other contacts you want to link. Once a checkmark appears, then it's selected.
- Afterward, select the **Menu button** ⋮ at the upper-right.
- Then choose "**Merge**."

Undo Contacts Changes

- Launch the Contacts app.

- From there, select the **Switch account button** ⑤ at the top-right.
- Now, choose "**Contacts app settings**."
- Underneath the "**Manage Contacts**" header, select "**Undo changes**."
- Proceed by selecting an option; Yesterday, 10 min ago, Custom, etc.
- Afterward, choose "**Confirm**."
- Next, choose "**OK**."

View Phone Number

- Launch the Settings app.
- Now, select "**About phone**."
- From here, you can see the "**Phone number**."

Chapter Eight

Manage Account Sync

If you are not getting email and application alerts, go through the guidelines below to double-check your sync settings.

- Launch the Settings app.
- Then choose "**Passwords & accounts**."
- Go ahead and choose the affected account.
- Then choose "**Account sync**." Proceed by toggling on **sync settings**. The options you'll see will depend on the type of account.

To make the account sync apply to all types of accounts:

- Launch the Settings app.
- Then choose "**Passwords & accounts**."
- Proceed by tapping the "**Automatically sync app data**" toggle to enable or disable it.

Change Phone Brightness

- Launch the Settings app.
- Then choose "**Display**."
- Next up, choose "**Brightness level**."

- Proceed by adjusting the the slider as you like.
- Hit on the "**Adaptive brightness**" toggle to enable or disable it.

Change Display Settings

- Launch the Settings app.
- Then choose "**Display**."
- From there, choose "**Screen timeout**."
- Now, choose an option.
- After that, press the Back arrow ←.
- Next up, choose "**Display size and text**."
- Proceed by adjusting the slider for both the "**Display size**" and "**Font size**" options.

Reset Phone Network

If you're unable to send and receive email and also connect to the internet, then try to reset your network.

- Launch the Settings app.
- Then choose "**System**."
- Next up, choose "**Reset options**."

- After this, choose "**Reset Wi-Fi, mobile & Bluetooth**."
- From there, select "**Reset settings**."
- When asked, insert your lock type (PIN, password/pattern).
- When asked, press "**Reset settings**." to approve.

Enable Screen Rotation

Screen rotation enables you to display and use your device applications (although not all apps support it) in a horizontal or vertical view.

- Launch the Settings app.
- Then select "**Display**."
- Hit on the "**Auto-rotate screen**" toggle to enable or disable it.

Enable Screen Inversion

- Launch the Settings app.
- Then choose "**Accessibility**."
- Next up, choose "**Color and motion**."
- Now, select "**Color inversion**."
- Proceed by tapping the "**Use color inversion**" toggle to enable or disable it.

Enable Airplane Mode

Once you have Airplane Mode turned on, all mobile network services will be disabled. However, you'll still be able to use Wi-Fi.

- Launch the Settings app.
- From there, choose "**Network & internet**."
- Next up, press the "**Airplane mode**" toggle to enable or disable it.

Enable Notification Snooze

- Launch the Settings app.
- Now, hit "**Notifications**." proceed by toggling on "**Allow notification snoozing**."

Do Not Disturb Mode

On the "Do Not Disturb" menu, you can choose calls, messages, and applications that can send you alerts, while the rest will be blocked during the period in which Do Not Disturb is enabled.

Setting up Priorities

- Launch the Settings app.
- From there, choose "**Sound & vibration**."
- Next up, choose "**Do Not Disturb**."
- Go ahead and choose Messages, Apps, or People to customize the settings that can bypass the Do Not Disturb mode when enabled.
- Tap either of the following then select the appropriate options to edit the settings for what can interrupt the Do Not Disturb setting when it's turned on:
- Afterward, press the **Back button** ← and choose "**Schedules**" to schedule Do Not Disturb.
- Go ahead and press the toggle next to "**Add more**," "**Sleeping**," or "**Event**." Then choose one.
- Hit on "**Days**," "**Start time**," and other options to customize them.
- Then press the **Back button** ← and select "**Turn on now**."
- If you need to turn it off instantly, press "**Turn off now**."

Adjust DND Settings

- Start by swiping downward two times from the top of the Home screen.

- Then choose **"Do Not Disturb"** to enable or disable it.
- Long-tap **"Do Not Disturb"** to show its settings menu.
- Hit on **"Duration"** and select **"For 1 hour"** or **"Until you turn off."**
- Press the plus or minus button ▬ to increase or reduce the timeframe.
- Then select **"OK."**

Set Date & Time

- Launch the Settings app.
- Then choose **"System."**
- Next up, select **"Date & time."**
- If you prefer to have your device time automatically set up by your network, choose either the **Set time** option or **"Use locale default."**
- To do it manually, ensure you've turned off the automatic options, then select **"Date."**
- Proceed by adjusting the date, then choose **"OK."**
- Next, select **"Time."**
- Proceed by adjusting the date, then choose **"OK."**
- Then select **"Time zone."**
- After that, choose **"Region"** and then choose your region.

- Next up, choose "**Time zone**" and choose your zone.
- If preferred, select "**Use 24-hour format**" to enable it.

Set up Extreme Battery Saver

Extreme Battery Saver enables you to restrict the applications that will be active or use only the important ones.

- Launch the Settings app.
- From there, choose "**Battery**."
- Next up, choose "**Battery Saver**."
- After this, hit "**Extreme Battery Saver**."
- Afterward, hit "**When to use**."

View Device ID

- Launch the Settings app.
- Now, select "**About phone**."
- From here, you can see the IMEI.

View MAC Address

- Launch the Settings app.
- Now, select **"About phone."**
- Move down to see the **"Device Wi-Fi MAC address."**

Chapter Nine

Find My Phone

If you need to find, ring, or remotely wipe clean your missing Google Pixel, ensure Find My Device is enabled on it.

Enable Find My Device

- Launch the Settings app.
- From there, choose "**Google**."
- Next up, select "**Find My Device**."
- Proceed by tapping the "**Use Find My Device**" toggle to enable or disable it.
- With this, you can now locate misplaced devices directly from the download Find My Device app or from the web version.

Erase a Device Remotely

This will remotely wipe clean your applications and settings for a misplaced device.

- Use a PC to navigate to the Google Find My Device and ensure you're logged in with the same Gmail account on the lost phone.
- Under your Google Pixel, choose "**Erase**."
- Once you're shown the "**Erase all data?**" menu, choose "**Erase**."

Lock a Device Remotely

This option enables you to add a password remotely to your misplaced device.

- Use a PC to navigate to the Google Find My Device and ensure you're logged in with the same Gmail account on the lost phone.
- Then choose "**Lock**."
- Proceed by adding a new password, then confirm and tap the "**Lock**" button at the lower-right.

Remotely Ring a Device

When you remotely ring a misplaced device, it will ring for five minutes. If it is in your current surroundings, you can locate it from the sound.

- Use a PC to navigate to the Google Find My Device and ensure you're logged in with the same Gmail account on the lost phone.
- Then choose "**Ring**."
- When the "**Ring device?**" menu appears, select "**Ring**."

Enable GPS Location

- Launch the Settings app.
- Then select "**Location**."
- After this, press the "**Use location**" toggle to enable or disable it.
- When shown a disclaimer menu, select "**Agree**."

Chapter Ten

Change Wallpaper

- Navigate to your Google Pixel Home screen and long-tap an empty portion.
- Next up, choose "**Wallpaper & style**."
- Hit on "**Change wallpaper**."

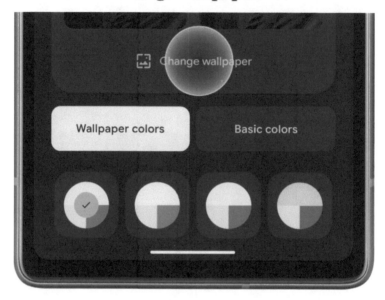

- Follow up by selecting a category. If you prefer to use your own image as a wallpaper, hit on "**My photos**."
- Go ahead and choose the photo.

- After that, choose **Done** ✓ .

Add Widgets

You can think of widgets as mini-applications that can be displayed on your home screen to show certain information.

- Navigate to your Google Pixel Home screen and long-tap an empty portion.
- Then choose "**Widgets**."
- Proceed by choosing a category, then long-tap a widget
- Follow up by dragging the widget to your desired Home screen and let go. Ensure the section has enough space.

Add a Folder

- Navigate to your Google Pixel Home screen and long-tap an app.
- Proceed by dragging the application onto another app, then let go.
- You'll now see a folder that contains the shortcuts. To rename it, click on it, then press the title box and insert a name. After that, select the Done button.
- If you need to remove a folder, start by dragging the applications out of it until the folder is no more.

Delete Apps & Widgets

- On your phone's Home screen, long-tap an app or widget.
- Proceed by dragging the app/widget to "**Remove**," which is positioned at the top then let go.

Enable Screen Protector Mode

Once you enable this, your screen sensitivity will increase.

- Launch the Setting app.
- Then choose "**Display**."
- Next up, press the "**Screen protector mode**" toggle to enable or disable it.

Setting up Lock Screen Notifications

You can choose to have your lock screen alerts for applications displayed or hidden whenever the screen is locked.

- Launch the Settings app.
- From there, choose "**Notifications**."
- Next up, hit on "**Notifications on lock screen**."
- Proceed by selecting from the displayed options.

Enable Multi Window

With multi-windows, users can split their Google Pixel screen to display different applications on each side. However, not all applications support this.

- While on your Home screen, swipe upward and press from the bottom to reveal all open applications.
- Proceed by scrolling horizontally (left/right) to find your desired app.
- Then press the app icon positioned at the top.

- Next up, select "**Split top.**" What will be displayed may be different depending on the chosen application.

- Select the second application you intend to view from the Recent Apps menu.
- If you need to swap to another app, swipe upward and long-tap the bottom of the screen to reveal the open applications, then choose the needed app.
- If you need to exit the split screen, go ahead and slide the horizontal bar from top to bottom.

Enable the Accessibility Menu

The Accessibility Menu provides users with a big on-screen menu that allows them to capture screenshots, launch notifications, access Google Assistant, etc.

- Launch the Settings app.
- Now, choose "**Accessibility.**"

- Underneath the "**Interaction controls**" section, choose "**Accessibility Menu.**"

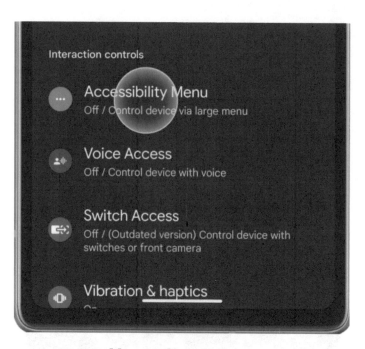

- Proceed by toggling on the **"Accessibility Menu shortcut."**

- Next up, choose "**Allow.**" You'll now see the accessibility button show up in the lower right of your display.
- Now, select "**Got it.**"

- Once you're set to use the Accessibility Menu, press the accessibility button.
- Hint: If you need to make the menu icons appear bigger, choose "**Settings.**" After that, toggle on "**Large buttons.**"

- Proceed by selecting an option from the menu.

Chapter Eleven

Perform Factory Reset

If your Google Pixel becomes unresponsive, applications begin to crash, and the keypad freezes, then you should attempt to troubleshoot by resetting it.

- Launch the Settings app.
- Next up, choose "**System**."
- Hit on "**Reset options**."
- After this, hit "**Erase all data(factory reset)**."
- From there, hit "**Erase all data**."
- When asked, insert your lock type, then hit on "**Erase all data**."
- Hold on for some minutes for the procedure to complete and for your Google Pixel to reboot.

Update Software

- Launch the Settings app.
- Next up, choose "**System**."
- After that, hit "System update."
- From there, hit on "**Check for update**."
- Now, hit "**OK**."

- If there's an available update, hit "**Download**."
- However, if you see the prompt "**Your system is up to date**," then there's no available update.

Add Ringtone

- Launch the Settings app.
- Now, hit on "**Sound & vibration**."
- After this, hit "**Phone ringtone**."
- Proceed by selecting your desired sound.
- Then hit "**Save**."

Enable Vibrate Mode

- Launch the Settings app.
- Now, hit on "**Sound & vibration**."
- Underneath the "**Ring & notification volume**" header, go ahead and slide the dot towards the left to make the Vibrate button show up.

Cast Phone Screen on TV

You can cast your Google Pixel screen on your smart TV. First, ensure that both gadgets are paired to the same Wi-Fi.

- Launch the Settings app.
- From there, hit "**Connected devices**."
- After this, hit "**Connection preferences**."
- Next up, hit **Cast** 📱.
- Proceed by choosing an available device to mirror your phone screen.

Manage Phone Storage

Once your apps start crashing or becoming unresponsive and you notice there isn't enough space, you can free up some space by deleting unneeded items.

- Launch the Settings app.
- Next up, choose "**Storage**."
- From there, you can see the "**Used space**."
- Now, hit on "**Free up space**" to start removing the unneeded apps and files.

Enable NFC

Near Field Communication, which is abbreviated "NFC," enables you to send files across another gadget that is just a few inches away, usually placed back-to-back, such as when making payments in a retail store.

- Launch the Settings app.
- From there, select "**Connected devices**."
- Next up, hit "**Connection preferences**."
- After that, choose "**NFC**."
- Now, hit on the "**Use NFC**" toggle to enable or disable it.

Set up Contactless Payments

Once you have NFC enabled and you need to make payment for your purchase, just bring your Google Pixel into contact with the payment terminal to approve payment. You can add Google Pay as your payment app.

- Launch the Settings app.
- Next up, choose "**Connected devices**."
- After this, hit "**Connected preferences**."

- Then select "**NFC**."
- Now, hit "**Contactless payments**."
- Afterward, hit on "**Default payment app**."
- From there, choose "**Google Pay**."

Add a default Message App

Once you add an application as your default SMS app, other messaging application features will be disabled.

- Launch the Settings app.
- Here, hit on "**Apps**."
- Now, hit on "**Default apps**."
- Afterward, hit "**SMS app**."
- Proceed by tapping your preferred SMS app.

Enable One-Handed Mode

One-handed mode enables users to conveniently operate their Google Pixel with one hand.

- Launch the Settings app.
- Next up, choose "**System**."
- After this, hit "**Languages & input**."
- From there, hit "**On-screen keyboard**."

- Now, hit on "**Gboard**."
- Afterward, hit "**Preferences**."
- After that, hit "**One-handed mode**."
- Proceed by selecting an option on the resulting menu.

Set up Printing

Before attempting to set up your printer, ensure it is paired with a Wi-Fi network

- Launch the Settings app.
- Now, hit "**Connected devices**."
- From there, hit "**Connection preferences**."
- After this, choose "**Printing**."
- Underneath the "**Print Services**" header, choose your desired printing option.
- After selection, a printer application might be downloaded from the Play Store.
- While on the selected service menu, toggle on "**Use print service**."
- Underneath the "**Printer**" header, choose your desired printer.
- However, if your desired printer isn't there you can add it.

Adding a Printer

- While on the "**Default Print Service**" menu, hit on the **Menu button** ⋮.
- Now, hit "**Add printer**."
- Proceed by choosing any of the displayed options.
- Hit on "**Add printer by IP address**."
- Underneath the "**Add Printer**" header, go ahead and insert the correct IP Address for your printer.
- Then choose "**Wi-Fi Direct printing**" to enable or disable it.
- After this, hit "**Find Wi-Fi Direct printers**" so that you can find the correct printer.

Chapter Twelve

Install Apps

If you need to install applications, books, games, etc., on your Google Pixel, navigate to the Play Store.

- Launch the Play Store app.
- From there, select the **Search button** at the top.
- Proceed by entering the application name into the search box. You can also navigate to the recommended content.
- At the bottom, you can also choose "**Books**," "**Apps**," "**Games**," etc.

- If you need to install an application, choose it and select "**Install**."

- To purchase a premium app, go ahead and pick your desired payment method, then select "**Buy**."

Manage your Apps

Just like other smartphones, your Google Pixel allows you to reorder your applications to your preferred positions.

Locate your Apps

While on your home screen, swipe upward from any portion of the screen above the search bar to reveal your device applications sorted in alphabetical order.

Move your Apps

If you intend to move an application from its current position to another location, long-tap the app's icon, then go ahead and drag it to your desired position, then release.

Group Apps

- Long-tap an application.
- Proceed by dragging the application on top of another one to create a folder containing the group of applications.

Remove Apps

- Long-tap an application.
- Proceed by dragging up the application.
- Then choose "**Remove**" to get rid of the application from the home screen.
- To completely remove the application from your Google Pixel, choose "**Uninstall.**"

Chapter Thirteen

Enable Live Translate

Live Translate enables users to translate words, road signs, websites, and more on their smartphones.

- Launch the Settings app.
- Then choose "**System**."

- Hit on "**Live Translate**."

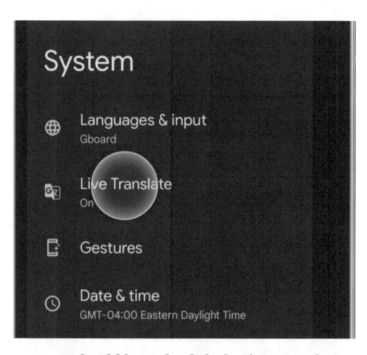

- It should be on by default, if not, toggle on
  "Use Live Translate."

- If you need to change the language you desire to translate to, hit on "**Translate to**."

- Go ahead and choose a language.
- From there, you will be shown the supported features for the selected language.
- Afterward, choose "**Select language**."
- If you desire to include more languages that you intend to translate, hit on "**Add a language**."

Using Live Translate

You can use the Camera application and Google Lens to translate what you want.

Google Lens

- If you need to translate languages that are displayed on your image, launch the Google Photos app.
- From there, choose an image.
- Then select "**Lens**."
- Afterward, select "**Translate**."

Camera App

With the Camera application, you can translate the words that are written on signs and menus.

- Launch the Camera app.
- Then choose "**Modes**."
- Hit on "**Lens**."
- Next up, choose "**Translate**."
- Long-tap the text you intend to translate.
- Then choose "**Translate**."

Add Motions & Gestures

The Google Pixel allows user to perform many motion and gesture movements on their devices.

- Launch the Settings app.
- From there, choose "**System**."
- Next up, select "**Gestures**."
- Proceed by selecting the displayed options such as **Gesture navigation**, **One-handed mode**, **Lift to check phone**, etc., and toggle them on or off.

Chapter Fourteen

Enable "Hold for Me"

Assuming you contact an organization and they put you on hold, you can ask the Google Assistant to wait and hold on your behalf and then inform you when the organization is available to talk with you. This feature is called "Hold for Me."

- Launch the Phone app.

- Then choose the **More button** ⋮.

- Afterward, choose "**Settings**."
- Next up, choose "**Hold for Me**."

- Go ahead and toggle on "**Hold for Me.**"

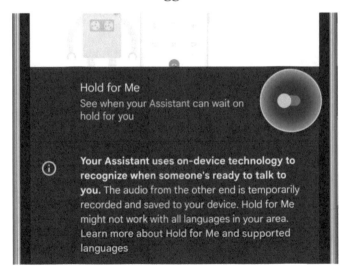

- Tip: after you've enabled Hold for Me, you'll need to also toggle it on for every call to inform the digital assistant to wait on hold on your behalf.

- Launch the Phone app and insert the number of the organization you prefer to call.
- If you're calling an organization, "**Wait Times**" will display the estimated duration you'll have to wait on hold before connecting.
- Hit "**Call**."
- Once you are put on hold, hit on "**Hold for Me**."
- Now, choose "**Start**."

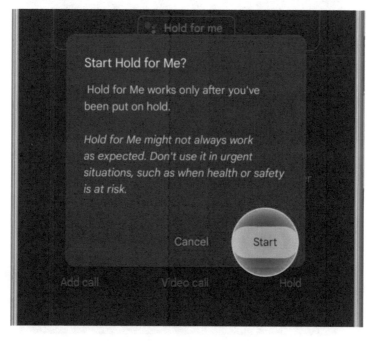

- For the duration you're on hold, your screen will display the "**Don't hang up**" option.
- Once the company's representative is ready to talk with you, you'll see the

memo "**Someone's waiting to talk to you**." Go ahead and select "**Return to call**" to return to the call.

Enable Direct My Call

If you contact a company that has an automated menu, you'll be shown on the screen the transcription of the automated menu and the menu options you'll need to select from via the clickable number buttons. This is made possible thanks to **Direct My Call**.

- Launch the Phone app.

- Then hit the **More symbol** ⋮ at the upper right.

- Afterward, choose "**Settings**."
- After this, choose "**Direct My Call**."

- Go ahead and toggle on **"Direct My Call."**

- If you're on a call with an automated menu and want to exit, hit **Close** ✕.

Manage Google Assistant

The Google Assistant enables you to control and navigate your Google Pixel phone by using voice commands.

Talk to Google

You'll be able to preview the languages that can be used with Google Assistant, start by saying "Hey Google, launch the Assistant settings." Below the "**All settings**," choose "Languages," then hit on "**Add a Language**." From here, you can preview the languages.

To trigger Google Assistant, long-tap the Power key of your Google Pixel. Alternatively, you can use the prompt; "Hey Google." Otherwise, press the Google mic button on your Home screen.

Get Update

To use the Google Assistant to fetch information or news, use the command; "Hey Google, tell me about tomorrow's weather." Or, "Hey Google, what's trending in the news today."

Play Media Content

Also, you can play/stream songs with Google Assistant, use the command "Hey Google, play my soul music playlist" or "play/stream a video on making crochet."

Add a Reminder

If you need to schedule a reminder, use the command "Hey Google, remind me to bake cake for the kids at 7 a.m. tomorrow." The voice assistant will enquire about some information from you, go ahead and follow the prompt.

Answer Calls

Once you enable Quick Phrases, the voice assistant can assist you with certain tasks, and you don't even have to use the trigger word "Hey Google."

If you need to enable Quick phrases:

- Start by saying "Hey Google, launch the Assistant settings."
- After that, select "**Quick phrases**."
- Proceed by tapping the toggle next to the phrases you prefer to use.
- After you've enabled Quick phrases and you have an incoming call, simply say "Answer" to answer the call or "Decline" to reject.

Adjust Settings

With the voice assistant, you can enable and disable certain features. For instance, use the command "Hey Google, enable Wi-Fi." This will turn on your Wi-Fi.

Set up a Routine

You can use the Google Assistant menu to set daily routines on your smartphone. For instance, you can set it to turn off your smart lights when you use the command "Hey Google, good night," and you can customize other routines to help you play videos, news, etc.

- To begin, use the command, "Hey Google, launch the Assistant settings."

- Below the "**Popular settings**" section, choose "**Routines**."

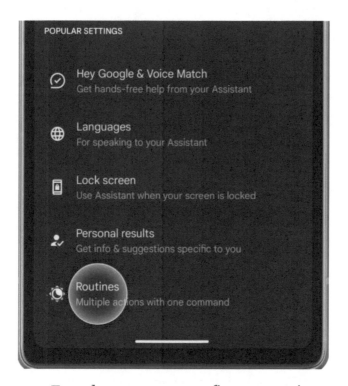

- From here, you can configure a routine or personalize an already existing one. Below the "**Your routines**" section, choose routine. For instance, if you need to configure a routine to assist you in getting your day started, choose "**Good morning**."

- Underneath "**Starters**," you'll be able to customize the commands that will enable the routine.
- Hit on "**Add action**" to insert an action into the routine.

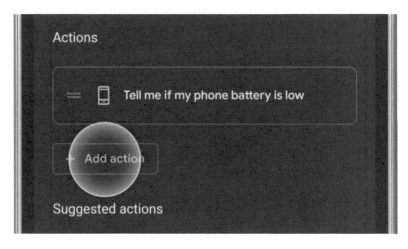

- Proceed by selecting the action you want the Assistant to execute whenever you speak the command. For instance, if you need to receive weather updates, hit on **"Get info and reminders."**

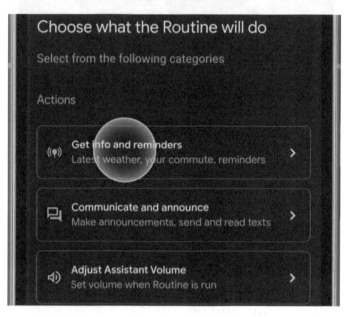

- Go ahead and select an option.

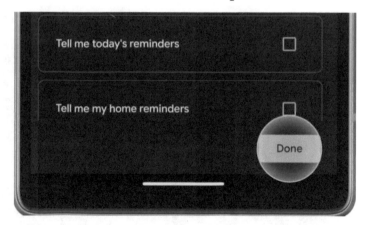

- Then choose "**Done**."
- Once you're done, hit "**Save**."

- With this, whenever you say the command "Hey Google, good morning," your Google Pixel will carry out all the actions that are associated with the routine.

Chapter Fifteen

Manage your Screen Time

With your Google Pixel, you can monitor and restrict the duration you spend while using applications on your phone in order to enhance your digital well-being.

- Launch the Settings app.
- From there, hit on **"Digital Wellbeing & parental controls."**

- From there, you will see a graph displaying your phone usage for the day:
- **Screen time**: this shows the applications you've used and for what duration.

- **Unlocks**: the number of times you've unlocked your Google Pixel.
- **Notifications**: this shows the number of notifications you've received.
- Proceed by selecting any of the options above to view additional information. For instance, choose "Notifications to know the applications that have sent you the highest number of notifications for the day.
- If you need to get additional data about the application displayed in the circle, click the application name.
- Hit on "**App timer**" to restrict the duration you spend in an application daily.

- Proceed by selecting the duration you prefer to use the app.
- Afterward, choose "**OK**."

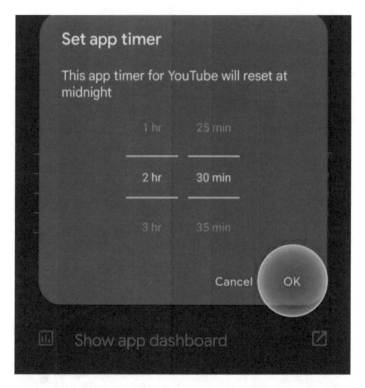

- Once the time you choose elapses, the application will exit and its icon becomes dark. However, the App timer will start over the next day.

Adding an Emergency Information

The Safety application on your Google Pixel enables you to include your emergency data, such as your medication, blood group, allergies, and emergency contacts, so that this information can be viewed on your phone lock screen during an emergency.

- Launch the Safety app.
- Afterward, choose "**Continue**."
- Next up, choose "**Your info**."

- Below the "**Emergency info**," hit on "**Emergency contacts**."

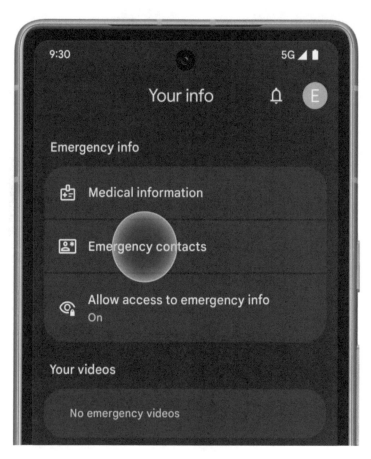

- After this, hit "**Add contact**."

- Proceed by selecting the person's name whom you intend to use as your emergency contact.
- If you need to add additional emergency contacts, hit on "**Add contact**" once more.
- Once you're done, press **Back** ⬅.
- Underneath the "**Emergency info**" heading, hit on "**Medical information**."

- Follow up by inserting any medical data you desire to appear on your Google Pixel lock screen during an emergency, such as drugs, blood group, or allergies.

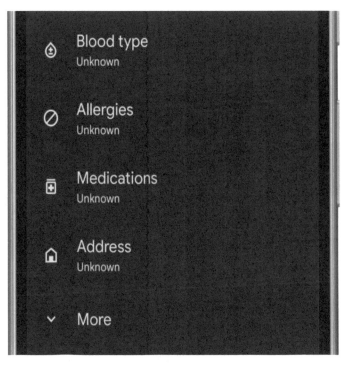

- Now press **Back** ←.

Share your Data during an Emergency

During an emergency, you can speedily share your location and other information with your emergency contacts. Ensure you have an internet connection and have added an emergency contact before you proceed to share.

- Launch the Safety app.

- If you've not configured Emergency sharing, you will be asked to do it first. Go through the procedure to permit location sharing and choose your emergency contact(s).
- After that, hit "**Emergency sharing**."

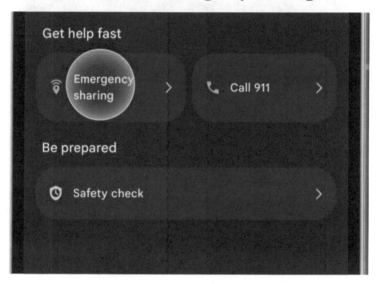

- However, if location sharing isn't available in your region, a memo will be displayed in the application.
- Proceed by choosing the person you intend to share your location with.
- Hint: if you need to adjust your status updates, hit on "**Change settings**." During emergency sharing, you'll be able to send updates concerning calls and battery life.
- Now, hit "**Share**."

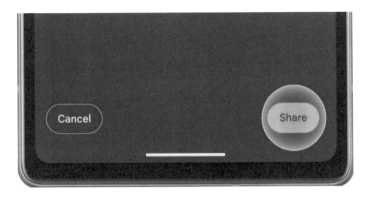

- Follow up by tapping the notification banner to reveal the information of your emergency sharing.
- If you need to stop sharing, hit "**Stop**," then approve by selecting "**Stop sharing**."

- If desired, you can insert your reason for discontinuing the emergency share, then choose "**Done**."
- However, your Emergency sharing will elapse after twenty-four hours.

Enable Safety Check

In the event that you're wandering around an unknown location, you can schedule a safety check so that your emergency contacts will be alerted if something goes wrong. Ensure you grant permission to Google Maps.

- Launch the Safety app.
- Now, choose "**Safety check**."

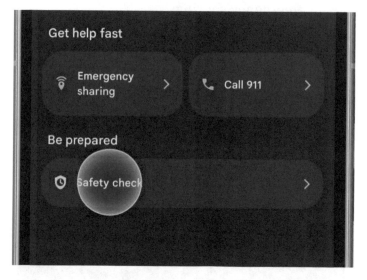

- You'll be asked to set up a Safety check if it's your first time. Go through the on-screen display to begin.
- Go ahead and choose your "**Reason**" and "**Duration**."

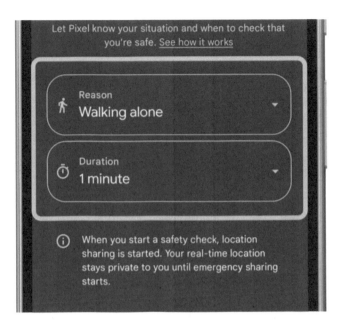

Let Pixel know your situation and when to check that you're safe. See how it works

Reason
🚶 Walking alone ▾

Duration
⏱ 1 minute ▾

ⓘ When you start a safety check, location sharing is started. Your real-time location stays private to you until emergency sharing starts.

- Afterward, choose "**Next**."
- Proceed by selecting your contacts.
- Next up, choose "**Start**."

Notify contacts when you start a safety check

Back   Start

- Once you enable alerts for your emergency contacts, they will be alerted whenever you set a safety check, including when it has elapsed.
- You will receive a notification once it's time to check in. Go ahead and select any

119

of the options below, depending on the situation:

- **Start sharing now**: this will terminate upcoming safety checks.
- **911**: This option will contact emergency services.
- **I'm OK**: this option will not share your location.
- If your smartphone goes off and there's no more signal, your safety check setting will still be active and will also commence an emergency share with your last identified location.
- However, if you do not select any of the above options within a minute, emergency sharing will commence. Your emergency contacts will get the URL to see your present location in Google Maps.

Enable Car Crash Detection

Once your Google Pixel detects a car crash, it'll automatically reach out to emergency services. For this to work, ensure airplane mode is disabled. However, your smartphone may not detect all car crashes.

- Launch the Safety app.
- Now, hit "**Features**."

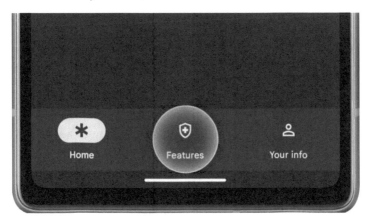

- Underneath "**Car crash detection**," hit on "**Manage settings**."

- Proceed by toggling on **"Car crash detection."** You may be asked to enable car crash detection; hit **"Yes, I'm in."**

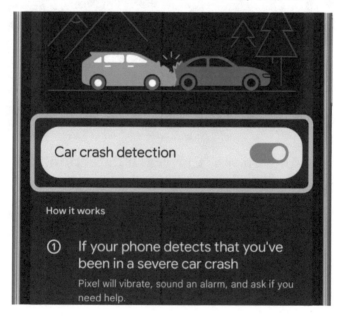

- Go through the on-screen guidelines to grant location permissions and other features.
- Once your Google Pixel notices that you're involved in a serious car crash, it'll issue a warning by vibrating and ringing loudly. It'll ask out loud and on display if you require any assistance.
- Tapping "**Cancel**" or swiping on the "**I'm OK**" option toward the right within one minute will cancel the call. Once you choose that you're OK, your smartphone will no longer contact emergency service.

- However, your smartphone will still ask if you're OK once more. Proceed by swiping toward the **No Crash** or **Minor Crash** option.

- But if there's a need for emergency services, go ahead and swipe the "**Call 911**" option towards the right.
- In the event of a serious car accident and you need to reach out to emergency services, use the voice prompt "**Emergency**" or select the Call 911 option.
- In case you don't choose any option within one minute, your Google Pixel will automatically call emergency services.

Enable Crisis Alerts

You can also get alerts on public emergencies such as floods, tsunamis, and more on your Google Pixel. Ensure the app is granted permission to your location.

- Launch the Safety app.
- Now, hit "**Features**."
- Underneath the "**Crisis alerts**," hit "**Manage settings**."

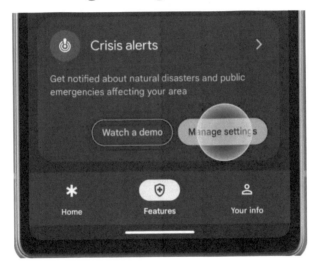

- Go ahead and toggle on "**Crisis alerts**."

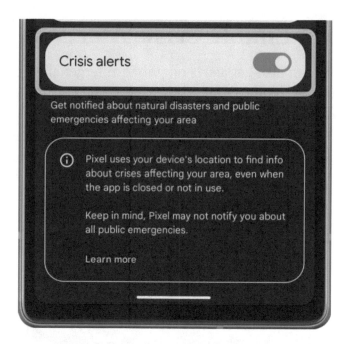

- Once there's a crisis alert on your smartphone, you'll see a URL redirecting you to the Safety application to get additional information.

Enable Emergency SOS

Your smartphone can contact emergency services when there's an emergency and even forward your location to your emergency contacts.

- Launch the Settings app.
- After this, hit **"Safety & emergency."**

- Next up, hit "**Emergency SOS.**"

- Proceed by turning on "**Emergency SOS**."

- An alarm will ring on your smartphone and it'll contact emergency services. To disable the alarm, disable the "**Play alarm sound**" button.
- Follow up by selecting the emergency service(s) you desire to enable.
- After you begin emergency SOS, your Google Pixel will kickstart the actions you configured.
- If you need to call your region emergency number, go ahead and enable "**Call emergency services**."

- If you need to adjust the number that is contacted, choose "**Number to call**," then insert the new number and hit "**Save**."
- Also, if you have to share your current location and report with your emergency contact(s), go ahead and enable  the "**real-time location**" button. Proceed by selecting other information to share.
- Follow up by enabling "**Record emergency video**" to commence an emergency recording. Go ahead and enable  "**Auto share**" to automatically forward your recording to your emergency contact(s).

- Once the menu asks you to allow capturing of audio, photos, and video, hit on "**While using the app**."
- If you need to kickstart Emergency SOS, press your phone's Power key swiftly five times or more.
- You should hear an alarm from your Google Pixel if you've enabled the countdown alarm. Swipe through the bottom of the display to discontinue the SOS or go ahead and swipe the "**Cancel**" slider.

Conclusion

The Google Pixel 8 series offers great features that you can optimize to help your workflow. Once you're done reading this user manual, you should be able to do amazing things with your Pixel smartphone.

About the Author

Shawn Blaine is a gadget reviewer, programmer, and computer geek. He has worked for some big tech companies in the past. He's currently focused on coding and blockchain development but still finds time to write and teach people how to use their smart devices to the fullest.

Other Books by the Author

- Amazon Echo Dot 5th Generation User Guide

https://amzn.to/40pJbC5

- Amazon Kindle 11th Generation User Guide

https://amzn.to/3HVRBK0

- iPad Pro 2022 User Guide

https://amzn.to/3l8xvUh

- iPad 10th Generation User Guide

https://amzn.to/3X5pSLk

- iPhone 14 Pro Max User Guide

https://amzn.to/3X6vEfM

- Kindle Fire HD 8 & HD 8 Plus (2022) User Guide

https://amzn.to/3DCWLbg

- Samsung Galaxy S23 Ultra 5G User Guide

https://amzn.to/43KQuFB

Index

15457884R00086